Networking:
The Skill the Schools Forgot to Teach

**What You Need to Know
to Get Ahead in Business**

By Cynthia D'Amour

Jump Start Books
Ann Arbor, MI

Networking:
The Skill the Schools Forgot to Teach

This book is dedicated
to Mom and Dad,
who never stopped supporting my dreams,
and, to my husband James,
for believing I could fly!
Thank you!

ISBN 0-9654600-0-2

To order additional copies of this book,
simply call, toll free:
1-888-994-3375

Acknowledgments

A book is not produced by the author alone. It takes long hours of input and work from many people.

I would like to take a moment to thank the following people for helping me:

To all of my friends and the people that I have networked with through the years. Your help and inspiration are the foundation of this book.

To all of the people who helped to review my rough drafts. Your feedback kept me on track.

To my editor, **Miriam Miller**. Thank you for making time for me. You were brave in your critiques and it really paid off.

To **Wendy Everett** of Publitech. Thank you for sharing your expertise and getting this book ready to print. It looks great.

To my friend **Cindy Jones**. Thank you for showing me how to get this to print and believing I could do it.

To **Michael Scott Karpovich, CSP**. Thank you for challenging me to leave my legacy.

And finally, to **my family and my husband James**. This book exists because of your constant and loving support. Thank you.

Table of Contents

Chapter One

What's the Big Deal about Networking?

Networking — It's Not Just for Sales People

There's a myth going around that networking is just for sales people. If you're not in sales, it doesn't apply to you.

Nothing can be farther from the truth!

Networking is a critical skill for anyone who plans to participate in life.

Networking is a human thing. It's about building relationships that are mutually beneficial.

Even cave people had networks. We just call them tribes. The cruelest punishment a cave person could receive was to be thrown out of the network.

Without the help of the network, survival was doubtful. The same is still true today.

We need each other to survive. There are very few people in our country who are totally self providing.

Most of us eat the food of farmers. We drive the cars that auto workers make. We work in buildings made by construction people.

The list is endless...

Why, then, is networking so hard to do?

Networking is hard because no one ever taught you how to do it. It's the skill the schools forgot to teach.

Why?

Teachers focused lots of facts and figures because you needed to score well on your exams.

Your grade point average, not your communication skills, determined your advancement in schools.

You didn't get extra credit for talking to your neighbor. Nobody cared what score you got for being a good listener or being skilled at conversation.

You had little, if any, formal training in building relationships or communicating with others.

And yet, once you became an adult, you were supposed to be great at networking.

After all, the best jobs are found by networking.

You're supposed to get lots of leads by networking and you may even participate in team sales.

You can build your career by networking within your current company.

Most business meetings even designate time for networking to take place.

HELP!!!!

No one ever taught you how to do it!

It doesn't have to hurt any more.

Networking is simply a series of skills that build relationships with other people.

This book will teach you no-fail, easy-to-use techniques for mastering these skills.

You'll learn how to confidently start conversations with strangers. How to mix and mingle with the best. How to stay in control of your nerves.

You'll also learn the process of developing a strong network and how to keep it growing.

The benefits of learning these skills will astound you and improve the quality of your life.

• You'll discover the confidence that has been hiding deep inside you.

• Your work will get easier and your stress load will decrease as your skills improve.

• You'll be able to get things done quicker and have more time on your hands.

It's time for you to learn these skills.

This book is designed to help you learn at the pace that's best for you. You can read it all in one sitting or simply take it one section at a time. It doesn't matter.

The key to your success is taking action.

What is Networking?

Before you jump into building your skills, you need to know what you're going to be doing.

Networking has many definitions for different people. Here are the definitions that we are going to use in this book.

1. Networking is about building mutually beneficial relationships with other people.

These are relationships in which both people do the giving and taking.

2. Networking is not limited to work.

You have a social network and a professional network. You have a network within any group that you participate in.

If you're active in many groups, people may say that you have a huge network. They're combining all of your smaller groups under one umbrella.

3. Networking takes time to see results.

If you're networking to grow your business, it may take you a good year to see real benefits of your actions.

People want to know that they can trust you to do a good job before they start referring you to others. You've got to keep showing up and staying in touch if you want networking to pay off.

4. Networking offers a variety of benefits.

You may get support, information, and friendship. You may also find mentors, people to mentor, and leisure time partners. Some even find a spouse.

Many people say networking is a great source for referrals. They're right.

If you take care of the people in your network, they may share business leads with you. You might also learn who are the gentle dentists, fantastic mechanics, and fun people to be with.

5. Networking is a way to add richness to your life.

It's a way to access information and events that you may have never discovered on your own. Your network can open many doors for you.

What Networking is Not About!

You've got some definitions about what networking is. Now, let's take a look at what it is not.

1. Networking is not attending a meeting and expecting everyone you meet to buy from you.

Meetings and networking events are NOT forums where sales pitches are supposed to be made. They are social relationship building events.

People want to mingle and have fun at these events. Save the sales pitch for a later meeting with those who are interested.

2. Networking events are not places to immediately increase the size of your sales force.

Just because you exchange cards with people, they have no obligation to refer you to anyone else.

Business referral meetings which require sharing leads are different than basic networking events. If you're at a networking event, these rules do not apply.

3. Networking is not another name for sales.

There is so much more that can be gained from meeting new people and building relationships with them. Making sales is just a tiny result of networking — and, it usually takes some time to occur.

4. Networking at events is not a painful form of torture that your company likes to require.

Networking is painful because you never learned how to do it. If you've been dreading these events for years, it's no wonder you call it torture.

As you learn the simple skills involved with networking, you'll feel like a new person. Attending these events will actually become fun for you.

Getting paid to have fun has a nice ring to it. Let's get you started on your path to success.

Your Most Valuable Networking Tool

The most valuable thing that you can offer people when networking is your name and its reputation.

When you promise to send some information, your actions reflect upon your name. Are you someone who keeps their word?

Is your name good? Can a person trust you?

When you refer a new mechanic to a friend, do they live up to your name? If the mechanic is a thief, it reflects on your name.

You need to be careful about who and what you attach your name to.

Pushy Paul doesn't like to waste time with small talk at networking events. His strategy is to distribute as many business cards as he possibly can.

He stuffs two cards in your hands without taking time to let you get to know him. He demands that you refer him to two of your networking buddies.

That's all he has to say. He's got more cards to give.

Do you feel comfortable risking your name by referring him to another contact?

Not if you value the importance of your name.

Your mother may have warned you when you were younger about your reputation. The same is still true in business.

Always tell the truth and only promise what you believe that you can do.

If you make a mistake, own it and make it right. Even the best can make an error. Your reputation will be more affected by how you handle it.

The more you grow your network, the more people will talk about you. You want that talk to be positive and trusting.

It's hard to change opinions once you lose trust.

This is a serious subject. But, if you start on the right foot, you don't have to ever look down again.

Make it a personal rule that your name will be the best that it can be.

A good reputation spreads good things back to you — it's your most valuable networking tool.

With your good name in hand, it's time to start working on your first networking skill.

The good news is, you don't have to leave your house to do it. Read on...

Chapter Two

Before You Leave Your House...

How to Be Socially Prepared

How would you like to go into any social event, whether for business or pleasure, and feel confident that you'll have some great conversations — even with people you don't know? Yes, it is possible.

The key to this success is to plan for it.

You need to know what's going on in the world around you. Be familiar with the big headlines.

Please note that I said headlines. Often times, people complain that they don't have time to keep up with all of the news. You don't have to know all of the details. You can always ask someone else for an opinion and learn from them.

You do, however, need to know the basics to be able to navigate. You'll also want to know how the home team is doing and any pressing local news.

There are many ways to learn the what the current headlines are.

It doesn't matter how you learn it. You can get your information from many sources such as radio, newspapers, TV, and the Internet.

If you don't like current events, relax.

You're not alone — but, you still need to know the basic headlines.

The good news is that learning about the headlines doesn't have to be "boring." Some radio stations have very funny morning shows that cover the news.

Listen to one of them for a few minutes and you'll be ready to talk to almost anyone.

You need to have a 2-3 topics that you find interesting to talk about.

Aside from current events headlines, it's also good to have a couple of pet topics that you feel confident talking about.

They can be anything from hobbies to human interest stories that you've heard.

Some examples of possible pet topics:

The information you learned on the Internet last night. The pig who was nursing a brood of puppies. Or, the tax tip that can save you $100s.

Your pet topics make conversations more interesting. They also make it easier for people to remember you the next day.

There are a few subjects that are still off limits — especially if you are talking to people that you don't know well.

They are sex, religion, and politics.

There's nothing wrong with any of these topics.

And, if you are at church, feel free to talk religion. If you're at a political function, talk about the greatness of your political party platform.

However, when you're out in the general public, avoid these three topics.

You'll find easier conversation and more acceptance by not bringing them up until you know your conversation partner better.

Being socially prepared keeps you ready to talk to anyone anywhere and still feel confident.

How to Prepare Questions for Easy Networking

Do you remember being in school and wishing that you knew what questions were going to be on the next day's test? The smart kids — maybe you were one of them — always seemed to know what to study and got good grades.

Whether you did well in school or not doesn't matter. You will be great at meeting new people because this book tells you what to study.

If you know what you're going to talk about in advance, you'll be prepared to have some great conversations with people you don't know.

You just need to do a little homework.

Am I expecting you to be psychic? Of course not. Do you have to memorize a bunch of stuff? No.

The secret to knowing the questions in advance is to be the one who asks them! It's just that simple.

When you first meet someone, there's often a bit of fumbling for a topic to talk about. You can use your questions to steer the direction of the conversation.

When you know what to ask in advance, you won't be as nervous about meeting new people.

So, plan your questions in advance!

Here's an example of how you can plan in advance.

If you know you have to attend a local chamber luncheon, find out ahead of time what the program will be. Who's going to be the speaker? What's the topic? What else is happening at the chamber or around town this month?

Using this information, come up with three or four open-ended, information-seeking questions. They should require more than a yes/no answer.

Some questions you might ask: What do you hope to learn from the speaker? What other books have you read on this topic? What did you think of them? What's your favorite chamber event to attend? Why?

These are good questions to launch into after you get beyond basic introductions. They are meaty questions that give people a chance to express an opinion and show off what they know.

Make sure you listen to what they say to you. You can learn a lot about the topic at hand as well as the person speaking. This lays a great foundation for your next meeting.

Meeting new people just got easier. You just keep asking the same questions. You'll feel more confident and be able to focus more on what they say.

Will people think you are strange if you keep using the same questions over and over? Only if you keep talking to the same people.

A Time Saving Technique

You can make up your conversation questions the day of the event or weeks in advance. Simply check out the event and jot your questions down.

You can keep them in your planner, on your computer, on your calendar... Just make sure you know where they are if you do it in advance.

If you get very nervous at these events, write your questions on a card and keep them in your pocket or purse. Then, if you see someone you really want to meet, you can pull your card out and review your questions before you approach them.

Some people feel more confident just knowing that the questions are with them.

A word of caution. Don't pull your card out in front of the person that you want to talk to. One man did, and got so embarrassed that he forgot how to read!

You may want to track your questions and their success. Some questions go over better than others. Keep using the good ones.

Will you have to make up questions before you go out for the rest of your life? Who knows. You may become a natural at asking good questions.

Or, you may become very good at asking questions you thought of ahead of time. Who cares — as long as you are feeling confident and having fun?

How to Get the Most Out of a Networking Event

The secret to getting the most out of a networking event is easy. Simply know what you want out of it before you get there. Set some goals.

The fantasy answer may be tons of sales. But we already talked about networking events not being a sales strategy target practice.

Networking is like dating. Your goal is marriage, but you've got to go on dates before it's a sure thing.

All right. So you're not going to walk out with a fist full of million-dollar orders. What else would help you to achieve your goals?

Is there any information that you need to know? People you meet can be incredible sources of valuable information. But, only if you remember to ask them for the answers to your questions.

Here are some of the things that I have learned at networking events: How to get free advertising for my business. (Which, by the way, led to me being featured on a three-day series on the local TV news.) Where to go for an honest tune-up for my car. The location of the best Chinese restaurant in town. The name of a printer who will go out of his way to make me happy.

This list can go on and on. I have saved thousands of dollars by networking. I have also made as much.

How can you tap into this gold mine?

Figure out what information will help you. Make a list of what you want to learn. Although some people use mental lists, it's easier to follow up when you use written lists.

Try to have at least two or three goals. Commit to asking the open-ended questions that focus on the information that you want to learn.

Use this technique every time you go out. You'll be amazed at what will happen.

You will start to get your answers. You'll also be more interesting to talk to. Why? Because you're asking some good questions.

The key to great conversation is not being a brilliant talker, it's asking good questions.

Later in the book, we'll get into how to actually work your questions into the conversation.

Visionary Networking for Bigger Results

One of the quickest ways for you to build your networking skills is to practice them in your head. Visualize yourself going up to someone you don't know and being successful.

You've prepared your three questions. See yourself introducing yourself. They are excited to meet you. You have an interesting conversation with them. Before you end your meeting, you swap information and plan to meet each other again.

Athletes all over the world run this type of "movie" in their heads to prepare them for their competitions. The same technique can work for you.

Stop for a moment. What are you saying to yourself right now? Do you have any resistance to visualizing the above scene in your mind?

If you don't, that's great. This is a very powerful technique and has helped tons of people improve their skills. It can help you too.

If you feel a little panicked because you don't know how to do this, relax. Later in the book, you'll learn easy-to-use approaches that will have you networking like the best of them in no time flat.

If you're not sure if visualizing will help you, that's fine. Try it out for yourself. See if it does make a difference for you. Different things work for different people. That's why there are tons of different approaches described in this book.

If you are thinking that there's no way you will ever be able to do the above scene with confidence, we need to talk.

Your mind is your biggest friend — and enemy.

If you honestly don't think that you'll ever be comfortable or any good at networking, you're right. Your mind will make sure that you have the experiences that will make you right.

A simple example. You and a friend are going to a party. You think it is going to be horrible and a big waste of time. Your friend is excitedly anticipating all of the fun that will be had at the party.

What happens at the party? You have a rotten time. Your friend has a blast. You attended the same party. What was the big difference? Your expectations.

You've got to be willing to believe that you can learn how to network. It's simply a series of skills. It may be scary and uncomfortable at times. But, wasn't riding a bike for the first time the same way? You'll get over the awkwardness very quickly. I promise.

Without thinking you can, you won't. I'm going to share with you simple no-fail approaches. Whether you succeed or not will be up to you alone.

Let's Get Pumped Up for Networking!

Since you're still reading the book, I'm assuming that you're at least open to being successful with your networking skills. Let's get pumped up!

This is one of my personal favorite exercises to do before I go into someplace to meet new people — especially if I'm the least bit nervous!

We're going to practice it right now. You can use this later when you need to calm your nerves and get excited about networking. Here we go...

I want you to pretend that we're watching the last basketball game of the season. The clock is ticking down it's last seconds. The score is tied.

Suddenly, a member from your favorite team gets possession of the ball. They charge down the court towards the basket. People are counting down the seconds. 5..4..3..2..

Your man shoots, and he scores!!! You have just won one million dollars!!

Let's add some action to the picture. Put your hands up in a "V" or victory formation. Start the scene again in your head.

The clock is ticking. Your man gets the ball. He's charging down the court. He's dodging the defense.

Start cheering him on. Feel the excitement build. 5...4...3...2.... He shoots. He scores!!! You have just won one million dollars!!!

I want you to yell with me, "YES!!! YES!!! YES!!!"

You've just become a millionaire!

If your blood's not pumping, read the scene over again and this time, yell like you really won, "YES!!! YES!!! YES!!!"

Gosh, doesn't this feel good? I feel pumped up just typing it. Who's got time to be nervous?

You can do this in the car before you go into a networking type event. If you really practice it at home, just doing the big "Vs" and whispering, "YES!!! YES!!! YES!!!" will get you pumped up.

What do you do if someone sees you in your car? Just tell them that you wanted to get the wrinkles out of your sleeves. I'm assuming you kept the car windows rolled up.

If you find your energy draining while at the event, you can recharge yourself with this same exercise. Simply go into the stall in the bathroom and run your basketball victory scene in your head.

Make sure you do your hand motions to access your energy. I suggest you do your "YES!!! YES!!! YES!!!" silently. Or, you'll soon become the talk of the party.

Maybe you could turn that into a good thing...

— Chapter Three —

How to Start a Conversation with Anyone

It All Starts in Your Head

A simple shift in your mind can quantum leap your confidence and ability to talk with strangers.

Not feeling comfortable starting conversations with people you don't know, can cause you to get nervous when you attend networking events.

You never know what to say. Your palms always sweat. You try to be invisible. You don't want to be there. You're feeling very stressed...

STOP!

If you're sending off panic signals throughout your body, your mind can't supply you with interesting conversation topics.

Your mind and body have kicked into overtime to protect you from the "danger" of meeting people who you don't know.

Your survival is top priority! Your mind and body know only two solutions — fight or flight. They are trying to get you to choose the latter.

You need to change the tape in your head.

You need to remove the one that associates meeting people with great pain. The second step is to replace it with a tape that believes that networking is an exciting and "safe" opportunity for you.

How do you make the switch?

Stop focusing on the stress involved with meeting people. Instead, shift your focus to your opportunity to learn new and exciting things.

Each new person you meet has a lifetime of experience in them — filled with fascinating stories and knowledge for you to discover.

When you meet new people, try to tap into this wealth of information. Pretend you're a reporter on the search for a good story. Try to learn at least one thing from each person.

Keep a log of the interesting things that you have learned. Make it a goal to add to your log every time you meet someone new.

Not sure how to do it?

You need to tap into the curiosity that you had as a child. You didn't worry if people liked you or not. The world was yours to explore — and you did it.

Go to your local mall and check out the play area in the center. Watch the little kids mix and mingle. It's natural. They have fun.

If a little child can do it, you can too.

Regain the curiosity you had as a child. Ask lots of questions. Focus on learning new things. Enjoy the process — it can be lots of fun.

Starting a conversation is natural. You don't need to get stressed out worrying about what to say.

Using a Prop is a No-Fail Conversation Starter

Okay, now that you're ready to start talking and learning, what do you say? The easiest way to start a conversation with someone is to use a prop — such as where you are, the picture on the wall, a book in their hands, the selection of bagels in front of you...

A prop can be anything. You're limited only by your imagination and observation skills. A prop is basically your excuse to start a friendly conversation with an information seeking question.

Why should you use a prop?

It takes the pressure off you and your conversation partner. You're not focusing on each other. Instead, you are addressing neutral territory.

If you don't find a common connection with the other person, you can simply move on.

Using with a prop will make you feel more confident. It's a polite way to start talking to people you find interesting.

What you talk about doesn't matter.

Just ask an advice or opinion question about a nearby prop. It's simply a starting point. Your conversation will flow from there.

Does it work?

Sue attended a networking event during the winter. She didn't know anyone and was nervous. She decided to focus on learning information and leading with a standard prop — the weather.

Sue approached a woman on the edge of the group, introduced herself, and asked how the woman was dealing with the extreme cold (the prop).

The conversation went from the cold to the dry air in both of their apartments. They traded information on humidifiers and parted.

Does this sound like a silly conversation? Sue's new friend was a high level official in the city — and, met people constantly.

When Sue needed some help later on, the official remembered talking about humidifiers with her. Sue got her help.

What you talk about does not have to be brilliant. Your goal is to build relationships.

Props can provide great opportunities to discover common interests and issues between you and your conversation partner.

Networking is not limited to business hours.

You can meet new people any time. Using props will help you to start conversations with ease.

Some examples of questions to ask about a prop.

At a Lecture/Class: What did you think about the class? Have you taken any other classes by this teacher? Did what they teach you really work? How? Why not?

At a Networking Luncheon: What does your company do? How do you find your clients? What do you like about your job?

At the Dry Cleaners: Is the line always this long? Do you think that clothes that have dry cleaning labels in them really have to be dry cleaned? What kind of results have you had with the bulk rate dry cleaning?

At a Bagel store: Have you tried any of the different flavors of cream cheese? What flavor do you recommend? What's your favorite type of bagel? Have you tasted any of their experimental bagels?

At the Mall: How does this work? Have you tried this? Do you like it? Why? Do you think this matches? Which one works better? Do you think this will shrink? How do I know which one is best for me? Do you think this is as easy to use as they claim?

A question about a prop is a great way to start a conversation anywhere you go. You are limited only by your enthusiasm and creativity.

The Picture of Small Talk

Would you like to be able to talk with someone for five minutes or five hours and never run out of things to talk about? It's easy to do.

You're going to learn a four-part picture that will help you to talk endlessly with people you don't know.

I'm going to describe each piece to you. I want you to picture this in your head as we go along. The more details you add to the picture, the better you'll remember it — which is important to do when your nerves start to hit.

Let's get going. Picture in your mind a big black shiny "X."

Make it huge. See the sun bouncing off it. Get the picture clearly in your head.

On top of this "X," I want you to put a house with a chimney on it.

It can be any type of house as long as it has a chimney on it. The house can be as big or small as you want it to be...castle, mansion, fishing shack... It does not matter. It can even be your own house.

What color is your house? How many windows does it have? What type of roofing? Remember, the more details you add, the better you'll remember this.

Okay. You've got a big black shiny "X" and on top of that is a house with a chimney. Can you see it?

Out of the chimney, I want you to see a tennis racket flailing around as if it's smoke. It never leaves the chimney. It just swings back and forth.

You can use any type of tennis racquet that you want. It can be a big head or regular size. What color is it? How about the strings? Can you see it?

Let's start in the beginning. First, you have a big black shiny "X." On top of the "X," is a house with a chimney. Coming out of the chimney, instead of smoke, is a tennis racquet.

Your tennis racquet keeps bouncing something up and down. It's a clock.

Your clock can be any kind. It can be a grandfather clock, an alarm clock, or a stopwatch. Does it have roman numerals, numbers, or LED readout? Can you see it in your head?

Let's go back to the beginning. First, you have a big black shiny "X." On top of the "X," is a house with a chimney. Out of the chimney, instead of smoke, is a tennis racquet. The tennis racquet is bouncing a clock.

Try and repeat the picture out loud without looking at the book. If you need to peek, read the description over again starting with the very first "X."

Are you having trouble "seeing" the picture?

You may want to read the description aloud so you can hear it. If reading bothers you, tape it and then listen to the tape while sitting in a relaxed position.

Once you have the picture in your head, you can talk to someone for five minutes or five hours! You will never be lost for what to talk about next.

What does this picture have to do with talking to people?

Each part of the picture represents topics to talk about. You can use them as an outline for your conversation when you talk to others.

The "X" represents where you are.

Remember the old saying, "X marks the spot"? The easiest way to start a conversation is to talk about where you are. Use those props!

The house represents where you live.

You might talk about the area you live in, community activities, or your actual house. You don't need to give out your exact address to strangers. But, you can definitely have a conversation comparing notes on the art of dry walling.

The chimney is just decoration — I couldn't think of any other way to logically bring in the racquet.

The tennis racquet represents what you do in your leisure time.

Talking about leisure time can give you great insight into a person. It also helps to build a stronger foundation for a relationship. As you probably know, a ton of business takes place on the golf course.

The clock represents current events.

You always need to know what's going on in your world. We've already talked about how to learn the headlines. This is where you use the information.

You now have a four-part approach that can be used in conversation anywhere.

Use this as a support to build your confidence. As long as you know the picture, you can hold your own in conversation with anyone.

Don't worry about having to memorize information for each set of topics. You can use this approach to guide you on what questions to ask next.

What if you skip a topic or mix up the order? Who cares? This is simply a tool to give you an upper hand in starting a conversation. You will always have the next topic in your head. You don't need to worry.

Now that you know what each part means, let's do it together one last time. First, you have a big black shiny "X." On top of the "X" is a house with a chimney. Out of the chimney, instead of smoke, is a tennis racquet. The tennis racquet is bouncing a clock.

Did you get all of it? You're ready to start talking!

Chapter Four

How to Keep the Conversation Going

The Most Important Question You Can Ask

Having a good conversation is about sharing information with another person.

In theory, this should not be difficult — especially when both people are speaking the same language. But it is.

Why?

Because nobody speaks the same language.

I'm not talking about a male vs. female problem. It's not an ethnic problem. Or, even a class problem.

What's the real problem?

You define the words you use based on your life experiences. No one has ever walked in your shoes.

Here are some examples of how common words can be defined very differently.

What do the words "great vacation" mean to you?

Do they mean camping or yachting? Seeing as much as you can of Europe or exploring one city? Or, do they mean something completely different to you?

What about the word "rich"?

What does it take for you to feel rich? $100,000 or food on your table every night? Does money have everything or nothing to do with you feeling rich?

Every word has a personal meaning. You can't assume to understand without getting clarification.

Does this mean that every word needs to be explained? Or, perhaps that we should give up talking entirely? Of course not.

You know that words have different meanings. You want an easy way to keep a conversation going. Why not ask questions to check out other people's definitions — and, make them feel important?

Here's the most important question you can ask:

What does that mean to you?

This question is great for getting insight and may even save you money.

When you're told that something is affordable. Simply respond, "That sounds great. What does affordable mean to you?"

You can also use it during introductions.

If someone tells you that they are a business consultant, keep the conversation going by replying, "What do you do as a business consultant?"

Many of the buzz words that fly around are the biggest offenders when it comes to multiple meanings.

Asking for clarification will help you to understand what is really being said.

Will people resent the question?

NO!! In fact, it often makes them feel like their opinion is important. You come across as a caring person and they feel good.

"What does that mean to you?" is a simple question that will do wonders for keeping your conversations flowing smoothly.

What to Do If You Forget Someone's Name

1. Skip mentioning their name.

Someone approaches you and says, "Hi Joe! What's new?" Just launch into the answer. Hopefully, their name will come with time.

2. Ask for some clue as to how you know them.

"Wow. It's been a while. When was the last time that we saw each other?"

3. Introduce them to a nearby friend and leave out their name.

"Have you met my partner? (They shake their head no.) This is my partner James."

James can then ask for the missing name. "I'm sorry. I didn't catch your name."

The key to this solution is that James needs to ask the revealing question. It's not the most polite way to introduce someone but it can work.

4. Simply say "Hi." Then grab your friend and say, "Look who's here!"

Hopefully, your friend will remember the other person's name — and, use it when they say hello.

5. Read their name tag.

Sometimes people get so nervous, they forget that at most professional events, people have name tags on. Be sure to check it out.

6. Tell them that you know who they are, but you just can't place them.

Don't feel bad if this happens. You usually know people within a certain context.

When you run into them in a different place than usual it can be confusing. For example, many people look very different in weekend clothes compared to how they look in work clothes.

7. Simply admit that you forgot it.

"I'm sorry. My mind is blanking on your name. Would you please remind me what it is?"

While all of the above solutions can work, this is the easiest way to recover from forgetting a name. Most people will just simply state their name. Give a simple thank you and just go on talking.

Everyone forgets a name now and then. It's really no big deal. Ease up on yourself.

When you do, you might get a pleasant surprise. Many people start to remember names when they don't worry about forgetting them. You can too.

The Rhythm of Good Conversation

Good conversation is like a tennis — both people have to participate in order to play the game.

Everyone takes a turn contributing and listening in good conversation. If one person does all of the talking, it gets boring for the listeners.

Think about our tennis game. Would you want to play if you never got to return the ball? Would you even need to be on the court for your "partner" to play? Would you search them out to play with you?

Doesn't sound like too much fun, does it? The same is true for conversation. In order to be enjoyable, both people need a chance to "play."

How to Add Some Rhythm

1. Speak in 30 second sound bites — especially around people you don't know well.

This is enough time to make a short point and still keep the other person's interest. As a general rule, when you talk longer than this, you tend to lose the attention of the your listener.

By limiting yourself to 30 seconds, they have a chance to respond. It gives them a reason to stay in the conversation with you.

What if you're a fascinating person who has a ton to say? Still take the time to come up for air. The other person will ask you for more information if they are interested. If they don't, it's time to change the conversation or move on.

Do you need to carry around a stop watch? Of course not. Just be aware of how long you talk.

An easy way to get a feel for this is to try it at home. Time yourself. How much can you say in 30 seconds?

Ask a friend to try a rhythm experiment with you. Each of you gets a maximum of 30 seconds to talk. Simply say, "Stop" at the end of your time.

It'll take some practice for you to get comfortable speaking in 30 second sound bites. But, it's worth it. People will find you much more interesting to talk to. Why? Because they get a chance to talk too.

2. Shift the topic of discussion until you find one that works for both of you.

If you have just met the person you are talking to, it may take a little effort to get the conversation flowing smoothly. Listen to the responses you get.

If you discovered a topic of common interest, great. Enjoy the conversation. If they're not enthusiastic in their response, simply shift to a different topic.

Think of each topic as a probe or test for common ground upon which to build a relationship.

It's not unusual to have to send out two or three probes before the conversation really takes off.

You may start out talking about the luncheon speaker, discuss the group who's hosting the function, and not hit pay dirt until you mention your marketing efforts on the Internet.

You never know which topic is going to launch a great conversation and start a networking relationship. As long as the person is pleasant, hang in there.

3. After you have shared information, ask for the same information from them.

If someone asks what you do, answer them. Then, ask them about what they do.

If you are asked for an opinion, answer them. Then, ask what they think about the issue.

It's a simple technique that keeps a conversation going. It also gives you a chance to learn about each other at an even pace.

Why is this important? Relationships are two-way streets. The best ones are built on a give-and-take basis. You set the stage for this with the first conversation that you share.

Good conversation has a rhythm to it. These three techniques will help you improve your skills in no time flat.

What to Do if You Say Something DUMB!

Every once in a while, it happens to the best of people — including you. You're meeting new people, speaking to your peers, or talking to your boss.

Everything is going well. Then, suddenly, out of no where, it leaps out from your mouth. Everyone was listening. You did it... You said something DUMB!

Now, what do you do?

1. If your words were rude or inappropriate, apologize immediately.

Sometimes, what you say can have multiple meanings. You may not even think about the "other" meaning until you say it.

Or, your words may innocently trigger an emotional response in your listener due to recent death or divorce in their life.

If either happens, simply apologize. If you need to, clarify what you meant to say. Then, go on. Dwelling on it only makes matters worse.

2. If you totally jumbled up your words, stop. Reclaim the language and go on.

This usually happens when you're thinking faster than you can speak. After you take a deep breath, smile and say, "Okay, let's get back to English." Simply pick up the point before your words got jumbled — and start over.

You could also be honest and say, "I hate when my brain goes faster than my mouth."

Getting words jumbled can happen to anyone. It's not a big deal.

3. If you truly said something that was simply dumb, own it.

You can be dramatic. Pause, put a big grin on your face and proclaim, "You know, I was up all last night thinking about that comment." Then, laugh at yourself, and go on.

Or, you can be surprised. Pause and with a laughing smile ask, "Did I really just say what I think I said? Okay. Let's try again."

No matter what the situation, a confident response is all you need.

Whether you need to apologize for being off color or laugh at the craziness of what you just said, stay in control of yourself — and, don't feel bad.

Your blooper just means you're human.

Chapter Five

How to End Your Fear of Rejection

You Are Not Alone

The top three fears in our country right now are the fear of death, the fear of public speaking, and the fear of talking to people you don't know.

An important part of networking is talking to people you don't know in public — even though you may feel like you would rather die.

Is it any wonder, that networking is so hard for so many people?

If you don't feel comfortable attending networking events, you're not alone.

Almost everyone gets nervous meeting new people — even those who seem outgoing and confident.

I guess, this could mean that you're "normal".

That's good, but, it gets even better...

When it comes to meeting new people, most individuals worry about what to say and being rejected.

This means that if you're brave enough to approach them, they'll be nice to you — and not reject you.

And, since most people worry about what to say, if you make a mistake or fumble, it's no major event. Actually, they'll probably be even nicer to you — because they hope you'll act the same way.

The fact that almost everyone is scared is a bonus for you — it creates a great safety net for your success.

You just need to take the first step. Say, "Hello."

How You Can Take Control of Your Mind

There are many techniques for dealing with fear. I'm going to share with you the most effective technique that I have learned. It can help you face your fears and feel confident networking.

The key to success is following each step. Your mind is in a rut right now. You need to bust out of it!

Four Simple Steps

When fear starts to hit and your mind begins to chatter with doubt, take control with these four steps:

1. Say to yourself, "Stop." Deny the truth of whatever your mind is saying.

For example, "Stop. I can talk to an important business contact and sound intelligent." Or, "Stop. I can talk to someone I don't know and not goof it up."

2. Prove to your mind that it is wrong.

Think back through your experiences for a specific example of when you've had success with a similar situation. Tell your mind about it.

For example, "I spoke to Joe Business at the networking event for fifteen minutes and had a great time." Or, "I've met several people for coffee in my life.

Remember Sally and Bob? I've been doing business with them for ages now."

3. Tell your mind what it is that you can do.

For example, "I can talk to people that I find interesting like that person over there." Or, "I can ask this woman for her business card."

4. The final step: Do it now!

Don't wait. There's never a perfect time. The more you tell your mind that you can do something *and* do it, the easier life will become.

Your mind may try to start chattering again.

Don't let it happen. Begin the four steps again. Command it to stop. Give another example of your previous success.

Or, you may want to give more details about your original story of success.

For example, "Stop. I can talk to someone I don't know and not goof it up. I met both Sally and Bob **and** asked them for a coffee meeting. I didn't die doing it and they both said 'YES.' I can talk successfully with this person too."

Then, do it.

If you keep this up, your mind's chatter about impending failure will eventually slow down.

Some people who use this technique find that the voice in their head shifts from yelling at them to politely asking, "Are you sure you want to do this? Just checking to see if you're still in control."

I'm not sure why our mind chatters this way.

I do know that once you start to take charge of your mind, your self confidence will soar.

And, since confidence attracts people and success, networking will become much easier.

Before you know it, you'll meet tons of people everywhere and fear will be but a memory...

What to Do When Panic Strikes You

You may still occasionally experience a little bit of panic. Your mind may go temporarily blank or your nerves may flare — in spite of your best effort to control your mind.

The best way to keep your panic in check is to be prepared for it.

Here are some ideas to help you stay in control and be confident when panic strikes:

1. Smile.

When you get scared, your body starts to get tight and shut down. The physical action of smiling will release chemicals in your body that will help you to relax — and, help your mind shift out of panic mode.

2. Keep breathing.

As your body clenches in fear, you may forget to breathe. Don't. Instead focus on controlling your breathing. Feel the air go in and out. Calm yourself.

3. Change your location.

If you're standing when panic strikes, I suggest that you and your conversation partner sit down. If you're sitting, stretch your legs and stand.

This is a good way to give your body and mind a chance to re-focus. If the event has no chairs, you could suggest that both of you grab some food. You may need to get creative.

4. Excuse yourself for a moment.

You may be talking to more than one person or unable to move due to the event.

If this is the case, you can always excuse yourself for a moment to use the bathroom, make an important phone call or get yourself something to drink.

Don't forget to be polite and offer to get refills for others as well.

Use this momentary break to get back on track. You may want to pull out your list of questions and read it over. This is also a good time to do the "YES!" exercise we worked on earlier.

You've had your break. Now, go back to your conversation smiling — and, don't forget their drinks!

5. Focus just on listening to what is being said.

Don't worry about what you will have to say, just listen. You may find yourself getting caught up in what you're hearing — and, forget about the panic.

What do you do if you still need more time and it's your turn to say something? Fall back on encouraging replies like, "That's interesting. I'd like to hear more."

With a green light from you, they'll continue to talk. There's no need for you to panic.

6. Leave the event.

Graciously excuse yourself. "It was nice to meet you. I've got to leave and catch an appointment." Then, leave the event.

Sometimes, just giving yourself permission to leave if you need to, makes it easier to stay.

If you do leave, congratulate yourself on how long you stayed — even if it was only for 15 minutes.

Next, identify what caused your panic. What were you scared about?

Now, make a plan of action about what you will do differently next time.

Do you need to prepare better? Do you need to read this book again? Do you need to do some practicing at less intimidating events?

Finally, make sure you do what you need to do.

Do not beat yourself up over leaving.

Remember, your first step was to celebrate your success. If you work your action plan, you'll do a lot better next time.

This was just a good learning experience for you.

7. Ask for more time.

If they ask you a question and your mind goes blank, don't choke. Just say, "Good question. I need a moment to think about that. What's your opinion?"

What they say may trigger your answer. If you still need more time, ask for some clarification.

8. Get a lot more time.

If you should know the answer, but you don't, stop. Don't panic. Be honest.

"I know this like the back of my hand, but for some reason, my mind is blank. Can I call you tomorrow with the answer to this question?"

Ask for a business card. Write their question on the back. Do it in front of them. It lets them know that you're serious and they are important to you.

Finally, make sure you follow up with the answer when you said you would.

Don't make a big deal out of not knowing the answer earlier. When you call, simply say, "Here's the information that I promised you last night..."

9. Stand on one foot.

When all else fails, start standing on one foot. Casually lift one leg off the floor enough to force you to focus on staying balanced.

Don't look like a flamingo.

Bend your leg only enough to lift it just a little bit off the ground. You may even want to touch the ground slightly with your toe for appearance sake.

You won't have time to be panicked when you have to focus on your balance.

You can even do this when you're standing in front of a room presenting. Try it out for yourself.

10. About your heart pounding...

Do you really want it to stop?

Maybe it's just a reminder that through the panic you are alive!

— Chapter Six —

Strategies for Your Networking Success

How to Have a Magnetic Attitude

Networking is really a combination of skills plus attitudes. You've already learned how to get rid of your old fears.

Now you're going to learn how to become a networking magnet.

People are attracted to confident people.

When you look like you're confident, you'll be better received by people and approached more often.

It's just that simple.

How can you appear confident when you're really a bundle of nerves?

Let's take it step by step.

First of all, you need to look confident.

Make sure that you stand tall. Head up. Shoulders back. Relax your face and smile.

Don't clasp your hands in front of you. Instead, keep them at your sides or behind you — unless, of course, you have something to drink in your hands.

You now have the basic body look of a confident person. You'll probably need to do some practicing — especially if you're not used to being confident. Watch yourself in the mirror.

How do you look? Try to look confident as much as you can. Any time you pass a mirror do a quick check. You want to make this feel like second nature.

Adopting the body look of a confident person will make you feel more confident as well.

The look is a good start. But, there's more to it than just how your body is moving.

You need to also project the "air" of confidence.

The way to achieve that air is one of the best kept secrets of confident people.

Here it is...

Confident people expect other people to like them — and, they do.

People will rise up to your expectations.

If you think that they'll like you, they will. If you think that they won't like, they won't.

Whatever you think is right.

Why does it work this way?

Because you also believe your expectations — and act appropriately.

If you believe that everyone will like you, you act that way.

You don't have to worry about being rejected. You are open to meeting people. You know that they'll be nice. You have the air of confidence.

Conversely, if you believe that people will reject you, you also act differently — you have to be prepared for their rejection.

Your guard is up. Every person you meet has potential to hurt you. Why bother talking to anyone — it's just going to be painful? You hate pain. You never meet anybody at networking events.

What a difference your thoughts can make!

Who do you think would be more fun to get to know? Which set of beliefs do you usually adopt? Is it time for a change?

If you don't believe the difference that your beliefs can make, test it for yourself.

Try out both mind sets. See if you notice any difference in how you behave AND how others respond to you.

What if you have a hard time believing that everyone will be glad to meet you?

Stop!

Why wouldn't they be glad to meet you?

You're interesting to talk with. (If you have any disagreement with this comment, you need to reread chapters two and three.) You know how to hold a conversation with anyone.

It doesn't make any sense that they wouldn't like to talk to you.

This is just an old tape playing in your head that you need to change immediately!

When you combine this positive attitude with confident body language, your networking experiences with change dramatically.

Think about it. You can become a networking magnet and you didn't even have to say a word...

How to Do the Business Card Shuffle

Networking is often associated with getting cards. It can also be a cause of great worry. How do you do it? What do you do with the cards once you get them?

Here are some tips to help you feel more confident doing the business card shuffle.

About handing out your card —

Don't worry about which side is up. Most people will automatically adjust it so they can take a quick glance at what it says.

Remember, you're exchanging cards for the purpose of future contact. The most important thing is to have a clean card with current information on it.

About taking notes on the cards you get —

You'll want to make some notes after you leave the event about the people you met. Your car is a great place to do this. Make it a habit to record information while it is still fresh in your mind.

On the back of each card, jot down the date and the name of the event you just attended.

Make note any other information that'll help you to remember them at a later date — such as conversation topics or outstanding physical features.

There's one exception to taking notes later.

If you promise to do something for a person, write it on their card in front of them. If you already know them, you may still want to ask for a card to make sure you follow through. Then, make sure you do it!

Do not overcommit yourself with promises of action in order to make a good first impression.

Your failure to come through on your word can brand you as a nice person who is not trustworthy.

This is not the kind of first impression that you want to make with your networking efforts!

About keeping your cards straight —

The easiest method to use is a two-pocket approach.

Keep your business cards in your right pocket. (Left handed people may want to reverse this.) Put other people's business cards in your left pocket.

Train yourself to do this and you'll never give out someone else's card as your own.

About remembering important contacts —

You may get many cards of varying value at a single event. It's important to be able to sort out the important contacts when the event is over.

The simple solution is to bend important cards.

As you put their card into your left pocket, use your thumb to bend the tip of the card.

This bend will become your secret signal to remind you later that the card belongs to someone who could be important to you.

Doing the business card shuffle is very easy when you have a system in place.

Later on, we'll talk about what to do with all of the cards you collect.

How to Get Answers to Your Questions

Earlier, you learned to set goals before you attend a networking event. It's now time to start getting answers to your questions.

People like to help others out.

Unless you are in a competitive position with someone, most people will enjoy the opportunity to help you get your answers. So let's get asking!

The first thing you need to do is set the stage for the your question.

Steer the conversation to the general topic that contains the answer you seek.

For example, you wouldn't ask for a referral of a good printer in the middle of a discussion about golf. It doesn't make sense.

It would, however, be a great time ask about a location for a golf outing.

How do you shift topics to get to the printer?

Wait until there is a break in the conversation. Then, use a transition like, "I have a business source question for you. Do you mind?"

They will almost always say "No."

If, however, their answer is "Yes," your timing was a little off. You need to respect their answer. Listen more carefully next time for a real conversation break.

If their answer is "Later," find out when a good time would be to ask your question. Follow up then.

Let's assume they say, "Yes."

Their mind is now shifted to business. Ask your question. "I'm looking for a good printer. Do you know any that you would recommend?"

If they answer "Yes," write down what they say. You may want to get some clarification about their suggestions. Ask them what they like about the printer. Find out what kind of projects the printer has done for them in the past.

Send a thank you note for the referral later.

If they didn't know any good printers, ask them if they know anyone who might.

This second question is getting you referral access to a third person's network.

Make sure you ask for permission to use their name when you call the referral. Most will let you if they gave you contact information.

Occasionally, they won't want their name to be used. Respect their wishes. You don't want to break their trust after they have just helped you.

Food for thought...

The information you get from networking can be incredibly valuable — and, sometimes totally wrong.

People may give you suggestions based on their best guesses because they like you and want to help.

You may want to get answers from a variety of sources — or, at least a second opinion. Use the information that fits you best.

You can continue this approach indefinitely. Simply continue to ask for specific information and follow with a request for contact.

Take good care of all of the people who help you — including your original contact and anyone who referred to you.

Thank you notes are a must.

They also put your contact information in the hands of your new friends for future reference.

If you ask enough questions, you will find the answers that you seek.

What are you waiting for?

Chapter Seven

What to Do in the First 15 Minutes

What to Do When You First Arrive

1. Go to the restroom or some place quiet.

Take a moment to compose yourself. Let go of the traffic and what was happening at work. It is time for you to focus. You need to be present in order for you to be a good listener.

You may want to quickly run through any questions that you planned for the event. What are your goals for the day? Tell yourself you are ready to carry on some great conversation.

Check yourself out in the mirror. Fix anything that got wind blown in the trip over. Check your teeth for food. Tell yourself you look good.

Stand tall and smile. Assume the stance of a confident person. You are ready to meet people.

2. Check in and get your name tag.

If your name tag is already prepared, look it over for any mistakes. If you need to, fix it.

If you have to make your own name tag, make sure you include both your name and your company name. Use the largest marker that they have. You want people to be able to read your name with ease.

Use this time to also check out who else is attending. Scan the prepared name tags. If the group provides an attendance list, make sure you grab one.

Is there any one coming who you really want to meet? How about people who you have met before and need to reacquaint yourself with?

3. Check out the location.

It's now time to officially enter the networking event. Scan the room's arrangement. Where are the other exits, if any?

Identify where most of the talking will take place. Where is the food located? How about the drinks? Are there any displays?

Is there dinner seating for later on? If there is, stay away from it until it is time to eat. Sitting down makes it very difficult for people to approach you.

You look good. Your name tag is on. You know the lay of the land. It's time to start talking!

How to Make an Unforgettable Introduction

The first thing you'll do when you meet new people is introduce yourself. Your introduction needs to help people remember your name and what you do.

Joe showed up regularly at almost all of the networking events in town. He talked to everyone. He even had his own name tag made.

After a year of showing up, Joe still wasn't getting the business from his networking buddies. In fact, several of them had ordered materials from a competitor who never attended anything.

Joe was frustrated. Why didn't they use him? He began to ask questions. What made his friends bypass him for the competition?

The answers he got shocked him.

Three of the people in his network had no idea what he did.

They knew his name and the name of his company. But, they didn't know what the company did. The name of the company was just someone's name.

Joe had never told them what he sold.

Joe was speechless. He thought that everyone knew what he did. He worked hard at networking. He had even given away hundreds of dollars in promotional trinkets with his contact information!

Joe's story is sad, but not unusual.

You've got to have a solid introduction if you want your networking efforts to pay off.

There are three key parts to a great introduction.

1. Your name.

Always give your first and last name. Say it slowly enough for the other person to hear it. If you have an unusual name you may want to provide them with a way to remember it.

For example, my last name is D'Amour. Because it's French, many people don't know how to pronounce it correctly. I simply tell them, "It's D'Amour — like D'More D'Better."

I don't use this example all of the time — just when people have trouble saying it. If your name has a similar challenge, you may want to come up with an easy reminder for people.

2. The name of your company.

You want people to know where you work. It gives them a better frame of reference about who you are. It's easier for them to come up with questions to ask you about. It's also easier for them to remember you when you see them later.

What do you do if you are between jobs and have no company to claim?

This is a great time for you to attend networking events. Many jobs are found by word of mouth.

When you introduce yourself, don't say that you're unemployed. Instead, tell them what you do in place of a company name. "My name is Susie Smith. I'm a mechanical engineer."

Their natural next question is to find out where you work. Your reply, "I'm currently between jobs. Do you know anyone who is looking for a mechanical engineer with 12 years of experience?" Smile.

You never know who people know. They may have just met someone else who was complaining about the shortage of good employees. Or, they may have no leads for you.

If you don't ask, you might miss out on a great job.

3. The final piece of your introduction is a short statement about what you specifically do.

It's like a one or two sentence infomercial. It helps the people you meet to understand and remember what you do.

Try to avoid the use of your industry's buzz words or words that don't mean a lot. Focus instead on the benefit that you offer people. Put it in simple terms that can hit home with anyone.

Don't be a desktop publisher. Instead, help people make more money with attractive newsletters.

Paint a picture with your words.

Test your description out on your friends and family. Even a middle school student should be able to understand your what-you-do statement.

As we learned from Joe's story, you can waste a ton of money and energy if no one knows what you do.

Work on your introduction. Practice it regularly. Be able to say it smoothly and comfortably. It's your verbal business card.

When do you use your three-part introduction?

Anytime you get a chance to introduce yourself.

Use it in small groups. Use it when everyone in the room stands up and introduces themselves.

Once you get the results you want from your introduction, stick with it — even if you get bored saying the same thing over and over.

People generally need to hear you introduce yourself at least seven times before they'll remember what you do and where you work.

A great introduction makes meeting people easier. It'll also make a world of difference in the success of your networking efforts.

How to Help Host an Event — Even if You Don't Know Anyone There

You are pumped up and ready to meet people, but how do you start? What do you do?

Instead of worrying about meeting new people and building a valuable network, pretend that you're hosting a party. Doing this will help you to take some of the pressure to perform off from you. You'll feel more comfortable.

What do you do when you usually host a party? You greet people. You help them get situated. You introduce them to others. You move around and spend time with all of your guests.

You have probably hosted a party before. It's not anything new. It's just using the same skills in a different location.

Do you need permission from the event planners to help host? Of course not. We're simply talking about your frame of mind.

However, if you belong to the group, you may want to offer to become a greeter. Sometimes the special name tag will build your confidence even more. If you're active in your Chamber of Commerce, check out becoming an ambassador for them. It's a neat opportunity to be an official host for the Chamber.

How do you "host" an event?

Start by standing just inside the doorway in the line of traffic. As people come in, greet them as if this is your personal networking event.

Put a big smile on your face. Extend your hand as you greet them. Make sure that you give your name.

Some people will simply say, "Hello," and move on. That's okay. You can catch up with them later.

They did not reject you.

After all, you wouldn't feel rejected if someone arrived at a party at your house, and felt comfortable joining right in, would you? Of course not.

Your mission is to make those less confident feel welcome and comfortable. Turn your attention back to the door and greet some more.

Most people will be thrilled to see a friendly face right inside of the door. You're making this meeting much easier for them.

How can you be nervous while helping others?

After you have talked to the first person for awhile, it's time to start moving. You'll learn the specifics of mingling later in this book.

Hosting the events you attend makes getting started very easy. Try it out for yourself.

Chapter Eight

How to Avoid the Most Common Networking Pitfalls

How to Handle Aggressive Sales People

Networking, in its pure form, is about building mutually beneficial relationships.

Unfortunately, it seems like a few people always view networking events as free-for-all, in-your-face sales opportunities.

After all, they have quotas to meet...

And, what better place for "cold calls" than a room full of people who are mingling? Or, so they think.

How do you graciously handle these inappropriate and misguided people?

Politely and firmly.

Sally Shoveit has read someplace that all she has to do to get more business is pass out her card to as many people as possible.

She comes to networking events with several inches of cards in her hands and immediately starts working the room.

When she approaches you, she might ask your name. Beyond that, it's a brief commercial about herself and her business.

She'll tell you why she is the only person to do business with — and then, takes an expectant pause...

Do you want to buy?

Do not flinch. Simply say, "I don't think so," and smile at her.

Because Sally's goal is to give out as many cards as possible, she will immediately leave you.

That is, after she's handed you 2-3 business cards — and, instructed you to give them to your friends.

Sally is a woman with a mission. As soon as you share your lack of interest with her, she'll move on.

Sally understands the value behind networking. Unfortunately, she has forgotten it's a two-way street.

She doesn't bother to find out what you do or if she can help you. She just passes out her cards...

Alvin the Obnoxious is a different story.

Like Sally, he has a big mission. But, instead just handing out cards, his goal is to make sales.

Alvin may be a little smoother than Sally. He's been taught to build a rapport before making his pitch.

You'll be casually talking with Alvin. It feels like real networking. You're on the path to discovering common interests with each other.

Suddenly, he will steer the conversation to what he does. Before you know it, Alvin has started into a full fledged sales pitch — and expects you to be ready to commit to him — on the spot!

What do you do if you don't want to buy?

Once you realize that he's giving you a sales pitch, you could interrupt him and ask, "Alvin, it sounds like you are trying to sell this to me. I really just came here for friendly conversation. Do you mind if we change the topic?"

He may apologize. He'll make a comment about being very excited about what he does — and then, ask for a good time to call you.

If you're interested in learning more about his product, give him a time to call.

If you're not interested in what he sells simply tell him. "Alvin, thank you for wanting to spend more time with me. I really don't see a need for your product right now and don't want to waste your selling time. But, I do wish you the best of luck with it."

This is an example of a sweet-sour-sweet rejection.

You thanked him. Told him you were not interested, and then you wished him good luck.

The first sweet is an acknowledgment of his request. It let's him know that you heard him.

The sour is the rejection.

The final sweet is a firm, but caring, confirmation that you're not interested.

This technique is very powerful. When you use all three parts, you appear to be a very confident and gracious person. Your rejection is kind.

Occasionally, Alvin will ignore your request to change the subject. Or, you may not have gotten a chance to say anything.

Alvin will try to close his sale with you. Simply use a sweet-sour-sweet statement to turn him down.

"Alvin, your product looks interesting. But, it's not a good fit for me. I wish you lots of luck selling it."

This should do it. If he's really aggressive, he might see your objection as just a maybe. He'll continue on with his sale.

At this point the easiest thing may be to simply end your conversation with him.

Always remember, YOU are in charge of who YOU spend time talking to at an event.

"Alvin, thanks for sharing your information with me. However, I'm not interested and have some more people to meet. Best of luck."

Shake his hand, and move on to the next person.

Alvin and Sally are not bad people.

They just don't understand that networking is about building mutually beneficial relationships — not making on-the-spot cold calls.

Networking events are a great opportunity for getting your foot in the door. When you follow up, people who you met are more inclined to see you.

Do not hesitate to hold your ground with Alvin and Sally. And, if you're interested in what they're selling, get together later.

It's time to move on. You've got people to meet!

Three Simple Solutions to Body Language Blocks

Many people block communication with their bodies and do not realize it. Here are the three most common blocks and simple solutions for quick results.

1. Make your face look approachable.

Most people are nervous about networking. What do they spend most of their time worrying about? If you will you accept them.

You want to be sure that your face says, "Welcome."

How do you do it? The easiest way is to smile.

Unfortunately, many nervous people look like they will bite off your nose. The message of their face is to STAY AWAY!

When you get nervous, your body prepares for danger and flight. Your face and jaw tightens. Your eyes may narrow. Your face does not look like you want to be approached.

People can read your face from across the room — and, respectfully stay away from you.

Do people regularly approach you at events? If they don't, you probably need to lighten up your face. Simply smiling more will make a big difference.

2. Use your arms to help conversation flow.

When you talk, make sure that your arms are to your sides or behind you. Don't hold your hands clasped in front of you. It makes you look less confident and less interested in talking to anyone.

If you are a "front of the body" person, simply hold them behind you. You'll need to train your body to accept this new position as normal.

It may take some work, but the effort is worth it!

3. Use your eyes to keep contact.

Eye contact lets the other person know that they are important to you. You care about their reactions.

But what if you're a person who needs to look into the air in order to think?

People expect you to look at them. Try to maintain some eye contact with them. Perhaps you can train yourself to look just over their head.

If you need to look away to process information, simply let them know what you're doing. "I'm not ignoring you. I want to give a good answer to your question, and I tend to think looking into space."

They'll feel better — and, you can think.

A few simple shifts in your body language can make a big difference in your networking success.

How to Solve the Challenge of the Cling-On

Networking is about meeting new people and building relationships. To be successful, you need to mingle and talk to several people at an event.

A Cling-On will challenge your success.

What is a Cling-On?

A person who stays at your side for an entire event.

They may try to monopolize your time and turn a mixer event into a coffee date. Or, they may simply follow you around like a lost puppy.

What if you recognize yourself in this description?

Don't worry.

All it means is that you need to work on your mingling skills. You'll learn how to do it with ease in the next section.

How do you gracefully get away from a Cling-On?

First, you need to understand what's going on.

Cling-Ons are hanging on to you because they feel safe. You're nice to them.

Why would they want to move on?

Besides, they don't really feel confident mingling at these events.

You're a life saver to them.

Be kind when you leave your Cling-On.

You can help your Cling-On by simply introducing them to someone new. Once the conversation is flowing, excuse yourself and move on.

This may be all it takes.

Your Cling-On is now safely talking to another person. You have helped to make the transition easier for them.

If your Cling-On follows you, it's time to talk.

If you like them, you can simply say, "It was great meeting you. How about getting together later in the week to talk more?" Exchange numbers.

"I look forward to talking to you again. Now it's time to get back to my networking goals. Enjoy the event. " Shake hands, smile and move on.

You have let your Cling-On know your boundaries. You both can look forward to your later meeting.

What if you don't want to meet them later?

Remember to stay kind — you never know who the Cling-On is friends with or related to.

If you don't want to begin a relationship with your Cling-On, simply go back a step.

Start talking to another person or group again.

Make sure you introduce your Cling-On. You can even steer the conversation to a topic you know they like to talk about.

This is your chance to leave your Cling-On. Just say, "Excuse me," and leave the conversation.

A Cling-On is a person who is not confident with their mingling skills — but, they may be a dynamite person to know and have in your network.

Your support will help them to build their skills and confidence. What a nice gift to share.

— Chapter Nine —

How to Mingle with Confidence and Ease

How to Approach a Group with Confidence

A key part of networking is mingling at events.

Approaching someone who is standing alone is very easy. All you have to do is smile, walk up and introduce yourself.

Approaching a group of people is a little different. It can be intimidating — but, it doesn't have to be.

The first thing you need to do before you approach a group is check out their body language.

If a group is casually socializing with each other, you have a green light to join them.

If the group is in an intimate conversation, you'll want to wait until later to approach them.

How can you tell the difference?

Use your eyes.

Closed circles, hushed voices, intense eye contact all indicate a serious discussion. This group probably does not want to be bothered. Move on.

It's time to approach the socializing group.

Put a smile on your face and simply walk up and join their circle of conversation. Make sure you step into the actual circle.

People will make room.

Kathy thought that she needed to be invited into a conversation before stepping into the circle.

Kathy was at a very successful event that she had coordinated. She was standing on the edge of a circle of VIPs that she had personally invited to the event.

She was very excited that they had showed. Patiently, she waited to be acknowledged.

Others walked up and just joined the conversation. They were accepted with no problem.

Why were the VIPs ignoring her?

The least they could do was thank her for all of the hard work she had done to make their day special. Kathy felt that she had earned that much...

The group began to break up. No one had said a word to her. Kathy was mad and frustrated.

Didn't they think that she was good enough?

The next day one of the VIPs called to thank her for the event. The only regret they had was that they didn't get a chance to meet her.

Kathy was in shock!

She had stood next to this person for close to five minutes!!! They never saw her — and, they had wanted to meet her!

Kathy learned a big lesson that day.

If you want to talk with a group, you have to become part of the group.

Step up. Join the circle of conversation.

How do you join in the conversation?

If the conversation doesn't break when you join the circle, don't worry. Just listen to what is being said and catch up on the topic.

If a point is being made, people will often wait for a break to greet you.

If you have something to add to the conversation, please do so.

You may want to throw a quick introduction in as well. "My name's Ken Jones from XYZ company, and I agree with what you said..."

Expect people to like you.

At these events, most people are very polite. Your input gives a new perspective and increases the value of the conversation for all.

If you're in a group and someone approaches, take the initiative to welcome them.

Ask for their name and share with them what your group was talking about. Be a good host.

Don't forget to use your questioning skills.

Even if you do not have an opinion, you can add to a conversation's flow with your interest. Ask for some clarification or another opinion.

Remember, good open-ended questions are just as important to conversation as information.

Now that you have joined a group, it's time to enjoy yourself and see what you can learn. Have fun.

How to Gracefully Exit a Conversation

When you attend a networking event, set a goal to meet at least three people.

This will keep you mingling at a nice easy pace — with plenty of time to get to know each other.

When do you move on?

When you have talked enough to find a common interest. At this point, exchange business cards. It's also a great time to suggest some future interaction.

To gracefully exit, simply use your sweet-sour-sweet combination. "It was nice meeting you. I need to talk to a few more people. I look forward to getting together later." Shake hands, smile, and move on.

Will they take offense because you want to talk to other people besides them?

No. You're suppose to be mingling. As long as you are kind in your departure, you are fine.

You're working on building a circle of friends — and, so are they.

Networking events are designed for starting new relationships and touching base with ones you have already started.

A word of caution.

Always pay attention to the person you are with.

One of the rudest things you can do is constantly scan the room for someone "more important" than the person you are currently talking to.

The only thing worse than this, is to interrupt the other person in mid-sentence saying, "Oh, Mr. Big is available now. I've just got to talk to him." And, run off without another word.

Does this really happen? Too many times.

Even if you do notice someone else that you would like to talk to, make sure you finish your current conversation. Put a nice close to the interaction. Then, pursue Mr. Big.

Treat everyone with respect. When you don't, word gets around about you. No one wants to deal with a shallow and rude person.

You need to mingle to make the most productive use of your time. But, always leave a conversation as gracefully as possible.

People tend to remember first and last impressions the best.

How to Get the Most Out of Eating Together

You've finished the social hour and it's time to eat. Who do you sit with?

Eating with people is really another hour of networking. The only difference is that you're seated.

Use this time to meet more people and get to know some new friends better.

There is always a great temptation to sit with your old buddies.

Don't do it!!!

A shared meal is an excellent chance to rapidly grow your network. People get to talk to you in a relaxed setting. They'll also remember you better.

During the meal, use your hosting skills.

Start out with people introducing themselves. This helps them to break the ice and gives everyone a voice at the table.

Ask questions of all of the people you're eating with — including those across the table. It's an opportunity for you to shine by making everyone feel included.

These questions can also help you to achieve some of your information seeking goals for the event.

Here are some round table questions that you might want to ask.

What marketing tip worked best for your business? What is the most unique way that you have prospected for business? Or, what was the weirdest way that a customer was referred to you?

What if someone doesn't respond well to your round table questions?

If someone appears to be a little stiff in their face, don't take it personally. They may just be nervous.

Sometimes, all they need is a little encouragement.

Make it easy for them to join the conversation. Ask them for a specific explanation or for an opinion.

Once in a while, the non-talker may pull back and seem to snarl. It's not about you. They may not feel well or are having a bad day.

You tried and were gracious. It's time to move on.

What about swapping cards?

You'll want to get the business cards of your table mates. Some people start exchanging the minute they sit down.

Your card will have more value if you wait. Start to lay a foundation of getting to know each other first. Then, share your cards.

Don't leave people out.

When the meal is ending, and you begin to swap, get a card from everyone. It's rude to leave someone out in this situation.

You may have found them incredibly boring. They may not be as skilled as you at table conversation.

Remember, you never know who they know. They may have a friend who needs your help. It's always good to be polite.

The paper clip trick will help your memory.

It's a nice touch to send your dinner partners a little note later on. You need to keep them separate from your other new contacts.

How do you keep them all straight?

Keep a paper clip in your pocket.

When you're finished collecting cards at the table, simply clip them together.

You won't have to worry about remembering who you ate with later. Now, you can relax and enjoy the rest of the event.

A shared meal is an opportunity for an hour of powerful networking. Use it well and watch your network grow.

Chapter Ten

What to Do the Morning After Networking

How to Make Yourself Stand Out From the Crowd

The difference between the average person and a dedicated networker is follow up.

We have already talked about making notes on the business cards that you received. It's now time to put that information to work.

Here are three things that you need to do to keep the momentum going in your relationship building.

1. Keep your promises.

If you have promised to send something to someone do it immediately. People remember your broken promises for a long time.

Donald met up with an old acquaintance who was in a new job and selling voice mail systems. The friend told Donald about some neat options that only her company offered.

He happened to be currently looking for a new voice mail service and asked her to send him some information. He was glad to be able to give business to his old acquaintance.

Donald went back to his office and told his business partner about the "gold mine solution" that he had discovered. Excitedly, he waited for the literature.

And he waited...

Donald held off from seeing other vendors. After all, this was his old acquaintance...

It never came.

Donald had embarrassed himself bragging about his great find. He even had another friend ready to convert to the new system. He felt betrayed.

That exchange took place almost two years ago. He remembers it like it was today — and, is still mad.

You can't afford to break down your network like Donald's acquaintance did.

Only make promises to people that you plan to keep — then do it!

2. Send "Nice to Meet You" notes.

Send "Nice to Meet You" notes to the people you met — and didn't promise to send anything to.

These are short one paragraph notes that will remind people who you are.

For example:

> *Dear Kathleen,*
>
> *It was a pleasure to meet you at the Chamber Marketing Luncheon yesterday. I enjoyed hearing about your new product debut. I look forward to seeing you again.*
>
> *Sincerely, Your First Name*

Make sure your contact information is included in the note. If it's not on the mailing piece, simply throw your business card in the envelope with it.

This note does two things.

First of all, it makes you stand out from everyone else. Very few people take the time to write these notes after an networking event.

The other thing it does is provide them with your information — just in case they didn't write in immediately on the back of your card.

You make remembering you easy to do.

What about sales literature?

If you promised to send literature, it should automatically be forwarded.

If they didn't request it, don't send it. The purpose of this note is to continue building your new relationship with them.

The note will help to build your trust level with them and make the sale easier. If this person is a hot prospect for you, follow up later with a meeting.

How will people remember what you do?

Your business card should read like a mini-brochure and explain what you can do. They already have your card in their possession.

Do NOT send a sales packet to everyone you meet.

Robert sent a complete kit including a video to everyone he met at a networking event.

The day that the kits arrived, the phones were buzzing about him. The comments were not positive.

Robert was referred to as a fool, unprofessional, and a money waster.

Who would want to do business with a person who was talked about like this?

Although Robert mailed the kits to people with best of intentions for his bottom line, it backfired on him. In fact, no one has seen Robert since then.

3. Add the new names to your tracking system.

Whether you use a contact base management program or a simple card box, you must have a system.

You need to track where you meet people and what you learned about them. You also need to be able to access their contact information with relative ease.

Find a system that works for you.

Make a commitment to follow these three steps every time you attend a networking event or meet someone for the first time.

If you keep it up, I promise your network will increase in returns dramatically with time.

Become Unforgettable with Thank You Notes

When you were younger, you were probably drilled on saying please and thank you.

The same rules are still true in business — but, very few people follow them.

Being a good thank you writer is another great opportunity to stand out as someone who cares.

These notes also help to keep your network alive.

You can thank people for almost anything.

1. Thank people for their time.

The day is not long enough to all that we want to do. If someone takes time to talk to you, thank them.

You took them away from other work and they made you a priority. Acknowledge their gift.

2. Thank people for information.

The obvious gift of information is a referral. But, don't forget to appreciate time-saving techniques, trends that affect you, and brainstormed ideas that they shared with you.

They didn't have to tell you anything.

3. Thank people for physical gifts.

Don't forget to drop a line for trial products, lunch and coffee. They may not have cost much, but it doesn't matter. You are appreciative of the thought.

Every time you receive anything, write a thank you note. It makes people feel special because you noticed their effort to help you.

What type of thank you note should you send?

Sending thank you notes has never been easier due to technology. Using e-mail, you can reach people in mere seconds.

You might have a form thank you letter on your computer that you send out. Just make sure you personalize it every time you use it.

A personal handwritten note gets lots of attention.

A simple handwritten three sentence thank you is often more effective than a beautifully written full page computer generated letter.

Why?

Because it shows that you cared enough to take the time to write — and, very few people do anymore.

No matter which form you choose, the bottom line is to make sure you do it.

How to Give a Great Compliment

Giving great compliments is a fine skill to have. You earn a special place in a person's heart when you give one — but, it must be sincere.

It's also another way to strengthen your network.

A great compliment has three parts.

1. Identify what you are complimenting.

"That was good," tells very little to the receiver of your compliment. What was good? Get specific.

Try instead, "Your report was well written." Now, they will know what you are talking about.

2. Tell them what you specifically liked about it.

What caused you to want to compliment them? Using our same example, was it the way they wrote concisely? The use of easy-to-read tables? Or, how about the thorough picture that it presented?

What did you really like?

3. Tell them why you like it.

With the report, is it easier for the client to understand? Does it make widgets fascinating? What is the benefit that their work provides?

Which compliment would you rather get from your boss about your work?

"That was good."

Or, "Your report was very well written. I especially liked how you used color graphs to support your points. You've made it very easy for our client to understand how we can help their business."

Makes a big difference, doesn't it?

Here are a few more examples.

"Your presentation was outstanding. I loved how you added the cartoons to your overheads. You really made a boring topic come to life."

"You did a great job catering our meal. I especially liked the tacos. They made be think about my trip to Mexico last year. Your food really helped make our fiesta theme work."

"You handled that customer's complaint well. I liked how you did not talk down to them and always seemed confident that you would make things right. You made our customer service policy come to life."

Compliments like these work well during business hours — and at home.

"You did a great job of helping your Dad clean the house. I noticed that every single toy is in its place. I feel very lucky to have a son who is such a big help."

It will take practice for you to get comfortable using all three parts of a great compliment.

One of the best places to work on this skill is in your thank you notes. You don't have to think on your feet. And, you can get used to the pattern.

No more, "Thanks for the idea."

Instead, "Thank you for telling me how to get free TV exposure. Our company is in a real growth mode, and TV is a great way to let people know about it."

The only rule about compliments is that they must be sincere. You don't want to come across like a flake.

Give them only when you mean it — but, don't be stingy. Everyone loves this kind of feedback.

Giving compliments in front of others adds even more impact to what you say — as long as your timing is appropriate.

Great compliments feel good whether you say them in person or put them in writing. They are very powerful networking tools.

Chapter Eleven

The Best Kept Networking Secrets

The Secret to Building a Solid Network

The secret to building a solid network is to build it one person at a time.

Some people run around frantically trying to meet as many people as they possibly can.

Timely Tom allots precisely four minutes per person at these events. He allows one minute for each introduction and two minutes for small talk.

Tom has a timer that buzzes in his pocket when the time is up. He quickly asks to exchange business cards, and then takes off for the next person.

In a typical two hour networking event, Timely Tom will "meet" 30 people.

How many people do you think will remember him the next day?

To build a strong network, you need to get out of the frantic "got to get as many cards as possible" frame of mind that Timely Tom has.

All it does is make you nervous. And, the people you talk with may discount you because of your abrupt interaction with them.

Don't buy the quantity over quality argument.

If you need to collect names for a direct mailing, use a business directory or data base. It will get you the same results.

Don't call "panicked name acquisition" networking.

Besides, if you had a carefully built network, you would simply need to ask to get names.

Call up people in your network and ask, "Chris, I'm about to launch a new product that does.... Do you know anyone who might need this benefit?"

Let's say you only get one name from ten people.

And, because your network already identified the needy people for you, you close half of them. That gives you five sales.

How much time, effort and money usually goes into making five sales through direct mail?

A ton!!!

It makes more sense to spend your time and energy building a strong network. You just have to be patient for the payoff.

Even if you aren't in sales, your network is an invaluable source of information.

No one makes it alone. And, it's a waste of energy to be constantly reinventing the wheel.

Why not learn from the successes and misses of others? That's what networking is really about.

Real networking takes time. But — every person you meet knows an average of 250 people.

Say you set a goal of meeting only three people and lay a good foundation for a relationship with each.

If you build them into your network, you will eventually have the potential to access 750 people that they know.

Think about what this means...

If you add only three people each week to your circle of friends, by the end of the year, your network will reach **117,000** people!

Build your network one solid relationship at a time. You'll always come out ahead.

The Secret to Getting the Most Out of Your Association Dues

Associations are great places to build your network. Many of them also have hefty membership fees.

The secret to getting the most out of your dues is to join them carefully and get involved.

Shop around and visit groups a few times before you commit. Some organizations have outstanding membership drives and offer very little for the rest of the year.

Determine which ones you'll benefit from most. Find the best fit for your networking goals.

There are three basic groups of associations.

1. Members are people in your industry.

These groups are wonderful for your professional development. They'll help you to stay current with what's going on in your industry. You'll also develop a network of people who experience challenges similar to your own.

2. Members are people in your customer base.

Identify the groups your clients belong to and check them out. You can become a friendly expert resource for this group. It's also a valuable opportunity to hear feedback about products and their needs. You'll build a network of potential clients.

3. Members are the local business community.

You'll meet people from many different professions and industries. They can be a great source of referrals and opportunities for collaborating on projects. You'll build a network of business support.

Your local Chamber of Commerce is an excellent source for meeting these people. Your Chamber also has access to a ton of information that can help your business grow.

If you're serious about doing business, you should check out your local Chamber of Commerce.

You need to decide which groups work for you — then, get involved.

Paying dues and becoming a paper member is not enough to build your network. You still have to take the time and energy to build relationships.

Help out on committees. Offer to greet at the door. Find a way for association members to get to know you as a person. Don't just be a name on the roster.

The way to get the most out of your association dues is to get involved. When you do, you'll find the investment worth every penny — and then some!

The Secret of
the Best Time to Network

Many people limit their networking time to business hours. After 5 p.m., it's their time.

If you think this way, you need to remember that networking is simply about building mutually beneficial relationships.

Any time is a good time to add someone to your network. It doesn't have to be a "business thing."

You already know how to do it.

The secret is to be friendly and talk to people every where you go. When you find a common interest, trade contact information. It's not a big deal.

You can do this at PTA meetings, bowling alleys, and even grocery stores.

Use the same skills that you learned throughout this book. Be a caring host. Ask good questions.

Your conversations will tend to be more casual and focused on leisure activities.

What you do for work may not come out until much later. Don't worry about it.

Your goal is to build relationships — not to do business deals 24 hours a day!

Finding a good tennis partner may be a valued addition to the quality of your after work hours. A business connection may be merely a bonus — but it's not always necessary.

What if you want to develop business connections in causal settings?

Find out where the type of people that you want to meet hang out. Where do they work out? Where do they play golf or do leisure type activities?

You can learn this information by simply asking people. Ask for their recommendations. Ask what the best day is to go there.

Start to go to these places. There is no guarantee that you'll meet any one, so make sure that you can enjoy yourself as well.

Explore bookstore sponsored talks by authors that you find interesting.

Get there at least fifteen minutes early. There's usually a book signing table after the author speaks. Hang around, and meet your fellow listeners.

You automatically have something in common with them — the author and what they talk about. It makes starting a conversation very easy.

Most of the big bookstores have special events that go on regularly. From discussion groups to mixing events, they are fun and filled with interesting people.

You can even target people with specific interests when you go to a bookstore.

All you have to do is look at the books in that particular section. For example, people who read travel books tend to be interested in travel.

Seek out for referrals. If you're responsible for upgrading the accounting system at work, check out the books in finance section.

When you see someone who looks like they are interested in the appropriate books, talk to them.

To start a conversation, simply say, "Excuse me. I notice that you're looking at accounting books. I need a new system at work and am looking for a good book about them. Do you have any suggestions?"

If they don't know anything or don't want to talk, they will tell you that they have no suggestions.

However, if they know something about it, they will usually start to ask you qualifying questions. If they ask you something that you didn't know was important, ask why they asked that question.

Once you get your referral or information that you seek, thank them. Give them a business card in case you can ever help them out. Conversations like these often end up in a great networking relationships.

Networking at any hour can help increase your quality of life both in and out of work. Enjoy.

Chapter Twelve

How to Get the Most Out of Your Efforts

How to Turn People You Meet into Valuable Contacts

Meeting people and sending a short note or information is a nice gesture. But, it takes more than this to turn your casual meetings into valuable contacts in your network.

Think of it like planting seeds in a garden.

They need water and sunshine to grow. They will develop at different rates. Some may mature into beautiful flowers, mighty oaks or merely weeds.

You won't know what potential your networking seed has — unless you help it grow.

Here are three tools that you can use to help your networking contacts to develop.

1. Keep a file of interesting articles — especially ones about your industry.

Most people only have time to follow their own industry. You can be a valuable source of information.

For example, your trade magazine runs an article about how to write dynamite letters that get lots of free publicity for new products.

You could share this information with business owners, marketing people, and copywriters.

Keeping these files will help you to become a quick resource expert for your industry.

Why do you want to become a resource?

The more you help others, the more that will come back to you. If all you do is take, people will eventually get tired of giving to you.

Being a resource for information about your industry is just one way that you can give.

2. Keep a drawer full of different types of cards that you can send your network.

You'll want to include birthday, anniversary, congratulations and thank you cards. Keep a roll of stamps near by.

You want to make sending these cards easy to do.

People like it when others remember their special days. It lets them know that you care.

You may want to create some postcards for yourself to use. Postcards are usually the first things read and are quick to write.

No matter what format you choose, make sure that you have all of your contact information on them. You always want it to be convenient for your network to get a hold of you.

3. Create some sort of contact system for yourself.

Make it a point to call people and stay in touch with what is going on with them.

"Hi. This is Craig. I haven't seen you in a while so I thought I'd give you a call to see what's new and exciting with you. Do you have a minute to talk?"

Even if they don't have time to talk, you have brought your name back to the front of their mind.

When you do talk with them, take notes. If you have helpful information to send them, do it. You may even discover an exciting reason to send a congratulations card to them.

All three tools add up to friendly reminders that let your network know that you're out there and you care about them.

You've got to stay in touch in order to grow your network. It takes time and energy, but the fruit of your labor can be incredibly sweet.

How to Get the Most Out of What You've Just Read

You're at the end of the book. You've learned a lot about networking skills. You want to start building up your network.

How do you start from here?

Take it one step at a time.

If you have a lot to work on don't feel bad about it. Everyone has room for improvement.

Babies don't run marathons.

And, you shouldn't expect to become an expert over night. You are working on building skills. They take time and practice.

You may need to read all of this book or sections of it several times. Do it. This is your guide to success.

Figure out what you need to learn, and more importantly, where you currently are with your skills.

Pick one or two things to start working on.

Trying to do it all is like expecting the crawling baby to stand up and run a marathon with it's first steps. It just doesn't make sense.

You will set yourself up for failure.

Instead, be kind to yourself. Every step you take is one step closer to where you want to be.

You are going to experience a learning curve with each of the skills.

At first you'll be very aware of what you're doing and feel awkward with the words and actions. As you practice the skill, you'll begin to gain confidence — but, will still be very aware of what you're doing.

Only after lots of practice, will each new skill be natural. You'll do it without thinking about the process. You'll feel confident doing it.

The key to getting good at networking is to stick with it. Start at the level you honestly are at and take it from there. You're not in a race with anyone.

If you've never liked networking before, you'll want to start with the basics. Put together a new introduction for yourself. Practice it in front of a mirror or with supportive friends.

For your first networking outing, set a goal to smile and say, "Hello," to at least three people. You don't have to get into any major conversations. If you make your three greetings, you have achieved your goal.

The following week, start to stretch yourself. Try to introduce yourself to three new people that week. Work on your body language at home.

Stretch yourself a little bit each week. You can do it.

If you are more confident and comfortable with the basics, start with some advanced skills. You may start by focusing on your mingling or follow up.

No matter where you begin your work, just do it.

Action is your only guarantee of successful change.

Without action, you will simply have spent time reading an interesting book.

Developing your networking skills is a gift you give yourself and the world. As you reach out and touch more people, the walls that block are torn down.

The person you sent the card to may have felt that no one really cared. You touched him.

The stranger that you start a conversation may have been filled with fear. You reached out to her.

The networking skills that you have learned can build businesses, create wonderful friendships, and much, much more.

May your life be filled with rewarding relationships and lots of fun!

About Cynthia D'Amour

Cynthia D'Amour is a dynamite networking specialist who delivers powerful, high-energy, content-driven presentations.

A certified teacher with a degree in marketing, Cynthia has an unique hands-on style that gets big results for all of her seminar participants.

Cynthia is committed to making the world a better place be teaching people how to build mutually beneficial relationships with each other.

You can help her make the world a better place.

She wants you to write her and share how this book has affected your life.

What skills really helped you feel more confident? What would you like to learn more about? Do you have any success stories that will help others?

Please write to her at:

Cynthia D'Amour
People Power Unlimited
P.O. Box 130881
Ann Arbor, MI 48113-0881

Fax: (313) 994-0097
E-mail: damour@earthlink.net

Index

T

taking a break 49
taking action 4
taking control of your mind 45
taking notes 58
team sales 3
technique for dealing with fear 45
technique for rejection 74
thank you notes 96–97, 100
thanking people 96
three-part introduction 68
time saving technique 16
torture 8
touching base 85
tracking system 95
trade magazines 110
trading contact information 106
trust 9, 10
trustworthy 60
turning people you meet into valuable
        contacts 109–111
two-pocket approach 60

U

unemployed 67
unforgettable introduction 65–68
unforgettable with thank you notes
        96–97
using a prop 26–28
using questioning skills 84
using your arms 77

V

valuable contacts 109–111
verbal business card 68
visionary networking for bigger results
        19–20
visualize 19

W

what is networking? 5
what networking is not about 7
what to do
    if you forget someone's name 36–37
    if you say something dumb 41–42
    in the first 15 minutes 63
    the morning after networking 91–100
    when panic strikes you 48
    when you first arrive 63–64
what's the big deal about networking? 1
when panic strikes you 48
when you first arrive 63–64

X

X marks the spot 31